Artists in Their World

Georgia O'Keeffe

Ruth Thomson

FRANKLIN WATTS

LONDON•SYDNEY

First published in 2003 by
Franklin Watts
96 Leonard Street,
London EC2A 4XD

Franklin Watts Australia
45-51 Huntley Street,
Alexandria,
NSW 2015

© Franklin Watts 2003

Series Editor: Adrian Cole
Editor: Sarah Peutrill
Series Designer: Mo Choy
Art Director: Jonathan Hair
Picture Researcher: Diana Morris

A CIP catalogue record for this book
is available from the British Library.

ISBN 0 7496 4627 6

Printed in Hong Kong, China

Acknowledgements

Collection of the University of Arizona Museum of Art, Tucson. Gift of Oliver James 50.1.4: front cover c, detail 20b,
21 all © ARS, New York and DACS, London 2003. Photo © 2002 The Art Institute of Chicago. All rights reserved.
The Alfred Stieglitz Collection, 1949.745: 14. Photo © 2002 The Art Institute of Chicago. All rights reserved. The
Alfred Stieglitz Collection, 1949.717: 42. Photo © 2001 The Art Institute of Chicago. All rights reserved. Gift of
Georgia O'Keeffe to the Alfred Stieglitz Collection, 1969.835: 15 © ARS, New York and DACS, London 2003. Photo
© 2002 The Art Institute of Chicago. All rights reserved. Gift of Georgia O'Keeffe, 1987.250.3: 39 © ARS, New York
and DACS, London 2003. Tom Bean/Corbis: 7b. Bettmann/Corbis: 24, 25t, 26t. Brooklyn Museum of Art,
NY/Bridgeman Art Library: 31 © ARS, New York and DACS, London 2003. Burstein Collection/Corbis: 40 © the
artist. Christies Images/Corbis: 17t © Aperture Foundation 2002. Geoffrey Clements/Corbis: 9b. Collection Center for
Creative Photography, University of Arizona, Tucson: 32b © Trustees of the Ansel Adams Publishing Rights Trust.
Peter Cook/View: 41b. Corbis: 10t, 12c. Corbis: 30t © The Trustees of the Ansel Adams Publishing Rights Trust.
Courtesy of George Eastman House:The Alfred Stieglitz Collection. Purchased from Georgia O'Keeffe 18b; front cover
bc & 22 Lewis Hine/Hulton Archive. Fisk University Galleries, Nashville, Tennessee: 23 © ARS, New York and
DACS, London 2003. Indianapolis Museum of Art. Gift of Mr & Mrs James W Fesler: 33 © ARS, New York and
DACS, London 2003. Collection of the McNay Art Museum. Bequest of Helen Miller Jones: 13 © ARS, New York and
DACS, London 2003. The Menil Collection, Houston. Gift of the Georgia O'Keeffe Foundation, 94-55: 11 © ARS,
New York and DACS, London 2003. Milwaukee Art Museum. Gift of Mrs Edward R Wehr, M1957.10: 35 © ARS,
New York and DACS, London 2003. Tina Modotti/AKG London: 20c. Joe Monroe/Archive Photos: 38t. Montclair Art
Museum, Montclair, NJ. Florence O.R. Lang Acquisition Fund 69.4: 22t. National Museum, Stockholm/Bridgeman Art
Library: 9t. Philadelphia Museum of Art, Pa/Corbis: 17b. The Phillips Collection, Washington, DC. Acquired 1926: 19
© ARS, New York and DACS, London 2003. Roman Soumar/Corbis: 18t. Alfred Stieglitz/Corbis: 16. Neil Thomson:
26c, 28t, 29, 30b, 32t, front cover br & 34, 36, 38b. Through the Flower: 41t © Judy Chicago. Underwood &
Underwood/Corbis: 25b. Wadsworth Atheneum, Hartford. The Ella Gallup Sumner & Mary Catlin Sumner Collection
Fund 1981.23: 27 © ARS, New York and DACS, London 2003. © Todd Webb. Courtesy of Evans Gallery, Portland,
Ma.: 34b. © 1998 Whitney Museum of American Art, New York. Lawrence H Bloedel Bequest, 77.1.37 : 37 © ARS,
New York and DACS, London 2003. Adam Woolfit/Corbis: 28b. Jim Zuckerman/Corbis: 36t.

Whilst every attempt has been made to clear copyright
should there be any inadvertent omission please apply
in the first instance to the publisher regarding rectification.

Contents

Who was Georgia O'Keeffe?

The O'Keeffe farmhouse overlooked a vast, open expanse of rolling farmland, covered with snow in winter, patterned with seedlings in spring and sparkling with golden wheat in high summer. The O'Keeffes owned 1,700 square kilometres of land.

Georgia O'Keeffe was one of the most influential painters in 20th-century American art. She is perhaps most famous for her close-up paintings of flowers, and her near-abstract Mexican landscapes.

O'Keeffe was born on 15 November 1887, the second child of Ida and Frank O'Keeffe. She was the eldest of five girls in a family of seven children. Her father was a successful farmer in Wisconsin. He ran a dairy and traded horses and cattle, as well as growing crops. He also built the farmhouse where the family lived, just outside the village of Sun Prairie near Madison.

CHILDHOOD ON THE FARM

The O'Keeffe children grew up helping on the farm. After school, while the boys worked with the horses, the girls learned to cook, sew and tend the vegetable garden. For fun, they played in the haylofts and on the garden swings. O'Keeffe also built a doll's house and spent hours on her own creating a make-believe world.

▲ O'Keeffe at the age of 15.

TIMELINE ▶

15 November 1887	1892	1898
Georgia O'Keeffe is born on a farm in Wisconsin, USA.	O'Keeffe attends Town Hall School.	O'Keeffe and two of her sisters begin taking drawing lessons.

EARLY EDUCATION

O'Keeffe's mother, Ida, was keen to make sure that her children had as good an education as possible. She wanted her five daughters, in particular, to have the chance to learn a profession, at a time when it was becoming more acceptable for women to go to university and to work outside the home.

In the evenings and at weekends, Ida read adventure stories to the children and played the piano for them. O'Keeffe loved music and learned to play both the piano and the violin.

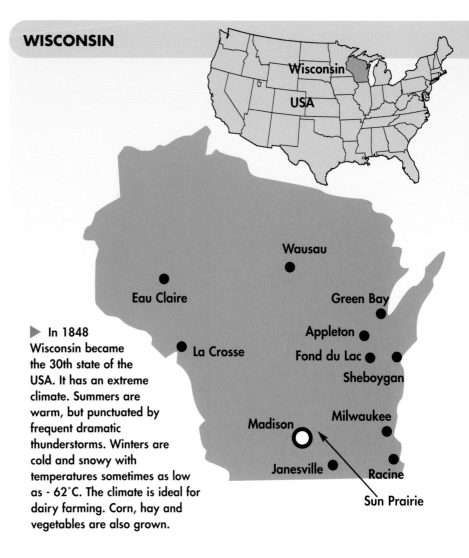

WISCONSIN

Wausau

Eau Claire

Green Bay

Appleton

La Crosse

Fond du Lac

Sheboygan

Milwaukee

Madison

Janesville

Racine

Sun Prairie

▶ In 1848 Wisconsin became the 30th state of the USA. It has an extreme climate. Summers are warm, but punctuated by frequent dramatic thunderstorms. Winters are cold and snowy with temperatures sometimes as low as - 62˚C. The climate is ideal for dairy farming. Corn, hay and vegetables are also grown.

▲ A view of the wide prairie of Wisconsin, where trees are scarce.

GOING TO SCHOOL

From the age of five, O'Keeffe went with other local farm children to the nearby one-roomed school-house, known as Town Hall School. She claimed later to have hated this school and not to have learned anything there. When she asked awkward questions in class, she was disappointed that her teacher couldn't answer them.

When O'Keeffe was eleven, she and two of her younger sisters began having weekly private drawing and painting lessons. The lessons consisted mainly of copying shaded cubes and pyramids, or imitating other artists' work, but O'Keeffe found them absorbing and progressed quickly. By the time she was 12, she had made a decision. 'I'm going to be an artist,' she announced to a friend.

Studying art

O'Keeffe's artistic talent was recognised at the various schools she went to during her adolescence. In 1901 she won an award for drawing at the nearby convent school in Madison.

The family moved to Virginia in 1902 and shortly afterwards O'Keeffe became a boarder at the private Chatham Episcopal Institute. There she was known as 'the queen of the art studio' for her skill in painting and drawing. The students elected her as art editor of the school yearbook. One of them was even inspired to write the following poem:

*'O is for O'Keeffe,
an artist divine.
Her paintings
are perfect and
drawings are fine.'*
Chatham Episcopal
Institute yearbook

▲ Wheatlands, the roomy white clapboard house that the O'Keeffes moved to in Williamsburg, Virginia.

STUDYING IN CHICAGO

In 1905, at the age of 17, O'Keeffe enrolled at the Art Institute of Chicago, where she learnt traditional art skills. Students copied casts of antique statues and studied rules of composition based on geometry. They studied anatomy and drew life models. Every month, the students' work was pinned up and ranked in order of merit. By the end of the year, O'Keeffe was ranked first in her class of 29 women.

When O'Keeffe went home for the summer in 1906, she fell ill with typhoid and could not return to Chicago. It took over a year for her to recover enough to consider painting again. Instead of returning to Chicago she decided to continue her studies at the Students Art League in New York.

TIMELINE ▶					
1902	Spring 1903	1905	Summer 1906	1907	1908-1912
Frank and Ida move to Williamsburg, Virginia. O'Keeffe remains in Madison with her aunt.	O'Keeffe joins her parents in Virginia. Enrols at Chatham Episcopal Institute.	O'Keeffe studies at the Art Institute of Chicago.	O'Keeffe is struck down with typhoid. She spends over a year at home.	O'Keeffe enrols at the Students Art League in New York where she studies under W. M. Chase.	O'Keeffe works first as a commercial artist in Chicago and later teaches in Virginia.

▲ *Dead Rabbit with Copper Pot, Quince, and Two Chestnuts*,
Jean-Baptiste-Siméon Chardin, 1739-40.
At art school in New York, O'Keeffe was taught still-life painting
following the traditional methods and compositions of past
masters such as Jean-Baptiste-Siméon Chardin (1699-1779).

STUDENTS ART LEAGUE

O'Keeffe enjoyed her studies in New York,
particularly the classes led by W. M. Chase
(see panel below). The school offered formal
art training following the European tradition
– painting portraits and still lifes.

However, in 1908, O'Keeffe's father's
business ran into trouble and she had to
drop out of the League. In order to make a
living, O'Keeffe became a commercial artist
in Chicago for two years. Then she taught
for several years in various schools and
colleges in Virginia.

*'I loved the colour in the brass
and copper pots and pans...'*
Georgia O'Keeffe talking about her
Chase still-life class

WILLIAM MERRITT CHASE

The teacher who impressed O'Keeffe the most was the artist
William Merritt Chase (1849-1916). He had studied in
Europe, where he was greatly influenced by Impressionist
painting. Chase painted with strong dark-light contrasts, thick,
swift brushstrokes and in warm, vivid colours. During his
weekly still-life classes, he demonstrated his skills, and then
encouraged his students to make equally bold, speedy and
lively pictures of their own.

Chase insisted that his students should paint a new picture
every day, and experiment with painting the same things in
different ways. He wanted them to understand that the actual
process of painting was more important than the final work,
so he made them paint eight or ten pictures one on top of the
other, until a canvas became too thick with paint.

O'Keeffe said about Chase, 'There was something fresh and
energetic and fierce and exacting about him that made him
fun.' At the end of the year, he gave her first prize for one of
her still lifes.

▲ *A Woman Reading*, William Merritt Chase,
c.1900.

Seeking her own way

▲ The suffragette parade in Washington D.C. in 1913.

In the summer of 1912, O'Keeffe enrolled on an advanced drawing course for school teachers at the University of Virginia. Here, her tutor Alon Bement introduced her to the ideas of Arthur Dow (1857-1922). His ideas inspired O'Keeffe to abandon the academic way of painting she had been taught.

ARTHUR DOW

Arthur Dow was a radical art teacher who taught for over 30 years. Inspired particularly by Japanese art, Dow believed that forms should be simplified, and that all the elements (colour, line, shape and volume) of a composition should be carefully arranged to create a balanced and harmonious design.

◄ Exercise No. 66, Arthur Dow, 1931.
This is taken from Dow's instructional book for students and teachers.

WOMEN'S RIGHTS

The National Women's Party was a militant group set up in the US in 1913 to win equal rights and the vote for women. They organised a massive suffragette march in Washington D.C.

O'Keeffe's friend Anita Pollitzer was a member of the National Women's Party and in 1914 she persuaded O'Keeffe to join. O'Keeffe, who believed that women should take responsibility for their own lives and earn their own living, kept up her membership for 30 years.

In 1920, the 19th Amendment became law, enabling women in the USA to vote for the first time.

After finishing her course, O'Keeffe began teaching in Texas, but in 1914 she returned to teachers' college, this time studying under Dow himself. With her creativity awakened, O'Keeffe went back to teaching, this time in South Carolina, and in turn inspired her students with the ideas she had learned from Dow. While teaching, however, she began seriously to consider a career as an independent artist. She started to experiment with abstract shapes that attempted to express her inner feelings. She made dramatic charcoal drawings using bold sweeping movements on large sheets of paper.

TIMELINE ▶

Summer 1912	August 1912-May 1914	Summer 1914	Autumn 1914-Spring 1915	September 1915
O'Keeffe attends the advanced painting class for teachers at Virginia.	O'Keeffe works as an art teacher at City Public School in Armarillo, Texas.	O'Keeffe joins the National Women's Party.	O'Keeffe enrols at Columbia University Teachers' College in New York. Studies under Dow.	O'Keeffe starts teaching art at Columbia College, South Carolina.

Early No. 2, 1915
charcoal on paper 61 x 47.3 cm The Menil Collection, Houston

During the early 1910s O'Keeffe wanted to concentrate on the formal elements of a picture – its lines, shapes and tonal values. To achieve this she worked exclusively in black and white as she felt that colour would be too distracting. She filled the paper with a few simple curved or geometric shapes, carefully balancing areas of light and shade. She later called some of these drawings 'Specials', to show how important they were to her.

First exhibitions

▲ O'Keeffe's first solo exhibition at the 291 Gallery in 1917.

THE 291 GALLERY

Alfred Stieglitz set up his 291 Gallery at 291 Fifth Avenue, New York. He held exhibitions of new-style photography, but also of African and modern European art at a time when it was not well known in America. Stieglitz was the first to show works by the French artists Auguste Rodin (1840-1917), Paul Cézanne (1839-1906), Henri Matisse (1869-1954) and Henri de Toulouse-Lautrec (1864-1901). He gave Pablo Picasso (1881-1973) and Henri Rousseau (1844-1910) their first solo exhibitions in the USA.

Stieglitz also promoted a select group of American painters, including O'Keeffe. His support was crucial in developing O'Keeffe's career as an artist.

In May 1916, O'Keeffe's friend Anita Pollitzer showed some drawings that O'Keeffe had given her to Alfred Stieglitz (1864-1946). Stieglitz was a well-known photographer and owner of an art gallery in New York, known as 291. He was hugely impressed and called her drawings the 'purest, finest, sincerest things that have entered 291 in a long time'. Without at first telling O'Keeffe, he exhibited the drawings in his gallery alongside the work of other artists. Although O'Keeffe was initially unhappy with this, she later forgave Stieglitz and they became friends.

LOVE OF NATURE

Later that year, O'Keeffe started a new job heading a college art department in the small town of Canyon, in Texas, where she applied some of Dow's ideas.

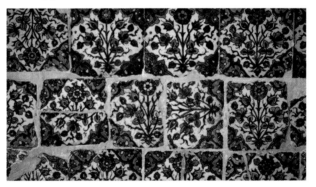

◄ Following Dow's exercises, O'Keeffe displayed pictures of Greek vases, Japanese prints and Persian patterns, like this one, to give her students inspiration.

O'Keeffe loved to explore her surroundings. She went on long walks across the wide prairie, where no trees, fences or surfaced roads interrupted the view. The landscape reminded her of the ocean with its vast, flat horizon and open sky. She enjoyed watching glowing sunrises and fiery sunsets. The vivid colours prompted her to use colour in her work again. She painted views of the canyon, sunrises and the planet Venus (see right). In 1917 Stieglitz exhibited O'Keeffe's watercolours and charcoal drawings in her first solo show.

TIMELINE ▶

May 1916	May 1916	June 1916	September 1916	November 1916	April-May 1917
Stieglitz exhibits O'Keeffe's charcoal drawings at 291.	O'Keeffe's mother dies of tuberculosis.	O'Keeffe begins to work using watercolours.	O'Keeffe heads the art department at West Texas State Normal College, Canyon.	O'Keeffe's works are included in a group exhibition at 291.	O'Keeffe's first solo exhibition at 291 – she sells her first charcoal drawing.

Evening Star V, 1917
watercolour on paper 22.2 x 30.2 cm McNay Art Museum, San Antonio, Texas
O'Keeffe painted eight versions of the planet Venus, the first 'star' visible in the evening sky. Without drawing first, she quickly painted a few shapes in vibrant colours, separated by bands of unpainted paper.

'I found I could say things with colour and shapes that I couldn't say in any other way – things I had no words for.'

Georgia O'Keeffe

A full-time painter

In 1918, O'Keeffe caught the flu, which was raging across the country, and she had to give up teaching. Her recovery was slow. Stieglitz, who had been writing regularly to O'Keeffe, became worried about her. He sent his friend, the photographer Paul Strand, to persuade her to come to New York.

NEW YORK ROMANCE

O'Keeffe arrived tired and ill. Stieglitz moved her into the vacant studio of his niece, at 114 East 59th Street. Day after day, they talked non-stop and soon fell in love. As O'Keeffe began to recover, Stieglitz started taking photographs of her, which clearly expressed his love for her.

In the summer, Stieglitz took O'Keeffe to his grand family house on the banks of Lake George in upstate New York. The surrounding countryside was lush and peaceful, with forest trails and flower-filled meadows. O'Keeffe spent the long days hiking, swimming, rowing and painting.

OIL PAINTING

At the end of the summer, Stieglitz asked O'Keeffe what she would most like to do if she could do anything she wanted for a year. O'Keeffe answered that she wanted to paint. Stieglitz persuaded one of his patrons to support O'Keeffe financially and she began experimenting with oil paints. Some of these early oil paintings were inspired by her love of music and her intense feelings about nature, such as *Blue and Green Music* (right).

▲ Stieglitz took many photographs of O'Keeffe's hands. She is shown here, sewing, in 1920.

STIEGLITZ'S PORTRAITS

The first pictures that Stieglitz took of O'Keeffe were close-up details of different parts of her body – her nose, lips, neck, hands, breasts, hips and hair. Stieglitz made more than 300 portraits of O'Keeffe, until he gave up photography at the age of 73. The later ones often showed her painting or standing in front of her work.

When Stieglitz first included 45 close-up portraits of O'Keeffe in an exhibition of his photographs in 1921, these daring works caused a sensation, drawing more public attention to her. People could see the happiness of Stieglitz in love. One woman visitor became tearful and, when asked why, said, 'He loves her so.'

TIMELINE ▶

February 1918	June 1918	July 1918	Summer 1918	November 1918	1919
O'Keeffe catches the flu and has to leave her position at Canyon.	O'Keeffe moves to New York.	Stieglitz moves in with O'Keeffe.	O'Keeffe spends her first holiday at Lake George.	O'Keeffe's father dies in an accident, falling off a roof.	O'Keeffe begins painting in oils. She visits York Beach, in Maine.

Blue and Green Music, 1919

oil on canvas 57.2 x 47 cm The Art Institute of Chicago

It is impossible to know whether this was painted in response to music O'Keeffe heard, or whether its title and colours refer to the sound of rippling waves and the windy woods at Lake George, where she painted it. It combines both natural and geometric forms.

'*Music that makes holes in the sky.*'

Georgia O'Keeffe

Stieglitz and his circle

▲ *Winter Night in New York,* Alfred Stieglitz, 1901.
This night-time photograph, with its dark, tree-lined path and globes of light in the distance, succeeds in capturing the eerie feeling of a freezing night.

By the time Alfred Stieglitz met O'Keeffe in 1916, he was the most famous photographer in America. Born to German parents in America in 1864, Stieglitz travelled with his family to Germany at the age of 17, and started to train as a mechanical engineer.

However, after buying a camera, Stieglitz became fascinated by photography. He changed his studies to photochemistry, set up a darkroom and a studio and started experimenting with photographic techniques. He was soon winning prizes for his prints in competitions.

STIEGLITZ'S PHOTOGRAPHY IN NEW YORK

In 1890 Stieglitz returned to New York. Here he bought a hand-held camera and roamed the city taking snapshots. He took photographs in the snow, the rain and the fog, and succeeded in taking the first-ever night-time photographs. He became as interested in capturing the atmosphere of a scene as in what it actually showed. He hoped people would understand what he was thinking and feeling by the way he shot his photographs.

PHOTOGRAPHIC ART

In 1903, determined to promote photography as an art in its own right, with the same status as painting, Stieglitz established a quarterly magazine called *Camera Work*. He also formed an association of photographers, called the Photo-Secessionists. They held exhibitions of their work at the gallery that Stieglitz opened in 1908, which later became known as the 291 Gallery (see page 12).

▲ *Wall Street,* Paul Strand, 1915. The strong geometric lines of this photograph are echoed in many of O'Keeffe's paintings.

▼ *Chinese Music,* Arthur Dove, 1923. O'Keeffe was drawn to the abstract paintings of Arthur Dove, whose work was inspired by nature.

CHAMPIONING AMERICAN ART

Towards the end of World War I (1914-18), Stieglitz decided to promote a small, select group of American artists – Arthur Dove (1880-1946), Marsden Hartley (1877-1943), John Marin (1870-1953), Charles Demuth (1883-1935), the photographer Paul Strand (1890-1976) and, later, Georgia O'Keeffe. They became known as the Stieglitz circle. Stieglitz opened several galleries, one after the other, and used them not merely to hold exhibitions, but also as somewhere to discuss his ideas about modern American art.

INFLUENCE ON O'KEEFFE

O'Keeffe's early years in New York were crucial to her development as an artist, and this was partly influenced by Stieglitz and his circle. These artists and photographers were all trying to find a new pictorial language to express their experiences of the American landscape and modern life. They rejected European influences and tried to create a uniquely American style.

Lake George

From 1918, O'Keeffe and Stieglitz settled into a regular routine. During the winters, they lived in New York. From late spring to early autumn, they went to Lake George. O'Keeffe spent the first part of her stay unwinding from city life – gardening, cooking, canning fruit or going on long walks.

During the second half of the summer O'Keeffe painted. She soon found, however, that she disliked the lack of privacy in the main house, where Stieglitz's relatives or guests were always coming and going.

THE SHANTY

O'Keeffe persuaded Stieglitz to let her use a wooden farm building as a studio, and this soon became known as 'The Shanty'. Here, O'Keeffe could paint in peace and guard her

▲ O'Keeffe painting in watercolour at Lake George in 1918.

privacy. She rarely allowed people to disturb her nor showed them what she was doing.

O'Keeffe's paintings were mainly based on nature, but she also painted some of the buildings around the property.

▲ A view of Lake George.

INSPIRATION AT LAKE GEORGE

The paintings O'Keeffe was inspired to do at Lake George were mainly landscape views of the lake or nearby mountains, close-up studies of leaves and flowers, or still lifes of ripe apples. The different coloured trees – birches, pines, maples, cedars and poplars – were also a favourite subject. She painted several pictures of the house and her shanty as well (see right). O'Keeffe's initial enthusiasm for the Lake George scenery and her happiness at being with Stieglitz is reflected in the paintings she did in the early 1920s.

TIMELINE ▶

February 1921	March 1922	Summer-Autumn 1922	December 1922
Exhibition of Stieglitz's photographs of O'Keeffe at the Anderson Galleries.	O'Keeffe designs the logo for a small literary magazine, *MSS*, produced by Stieglitz.	O'Keeffe paints at Lake George, including her first large landscapes.	O'Keeffe writes an autobiographical statement for an issue of *MSS*.

My Shanty, Lake George, 1922

oil on canvas 50.8 x 69.9 cm The Phillips Collection, Washington D.C.

O'Keeffe took over this old wooden shed, originally built for dancing, set in a field on a hill above the house. It had an outside platform where she often used to paint. Here she reduces the building to its flat, geometric shape and contrasts the rectangular walls and doors, the square window and the triangular roof with the organic shapes of the tree, hill and sky behind.

'O'Keeffe is busily painting. Primarily small things.
Very rich in colour. Oils and pastels.'

Alfred Stieglitz

Larger than life

In the 1920s O'Keeffe and Stieglitz continued their routine of visiting Lake George during the spring and summer. O'Keeffe started painting flowers in a way no one had ever done before. She focused on part of a flower head and magnified it so that it filled an entire canvas. The edges of the petals were often cut off. She painted flowers so large that they seem as close-up to the viewer as the flowers themselves might seem to a passing butterfly.

O'KEEFFE'S TECHNIQUE

O'Keeffe painted on canvas with a very fine weave and coated it with a special primer to make the surface extremely smooth. She subtly blended one colour into the next, making sure that the brushstrokes were invisible.

She simplified the form of the flowers, but carefully suggested their texture – whether waxy, velvety or soft. Notice the crisp lines of the petals in *Red Canna* (opposite and section below), and how the stronger tone along one edge of a petal helps to define its shape. It contrasts with either a pale or a different colour on the next petal.

◀ *Roses,* Tina Modotti, 1925. Photographers in O'Keeffe's time were also interested in close-up flower pictures.

▲ A detail of *Red Canna* (opposite).

CELEBRATING NATURE

O'Keeffe's flower pictures are often compared to photographs of natural objects taken around the same time. These also show plants close-up, in sharp focus and with cropped edges. O'Keeffe's interest, however, was not just in the plants and flowers themselves. By transforming them from small, fragile objects into huge, powerful ones, she was expressing her celebration of nature as a strong, vital force.

Over eight years, O'Keeffe painted almost 200 close-up flower pictures. Many were over a metre high. She painted both common flowers, such as poppies, daffodils, roses and sunflowers, and rarer specimens, such as black irises and red canna lilies.

TIMELINE ▶

1923	29 January 1923	March 1924	November 1924
O'Keeffe begins painting close-up pictures of plants and flowers.	Solo exhibition of 100 of O'Keeffe's pictures at the Anderson Galleries.	Joint exhibition of Stieglitz's photographs and O'Keeffe's pictures.	O'Keeffe and Stieglitz move into their first apartment.

Red Canna, 1924
oil on canvas mounted on masonite 91.4 x 76 cm University of Arizona Museum of Art, Tucson
The flower is so magnified that the petals appear to be an abstract arrangement of overlapping, uplifting lines and tones.

'I'll paint what I see – what the flower is to me but I'll paint it big... I will make even busy New Yorkers take time to see what I see of flowers.'

Georgia O'Keeffe

The high life

▲ *Queensborough Bridge*, **Elsie Driggs, 1927.**

O'Keeffe and Stieglitz married in New Jersey in December 1924 and late the following year moved to the recently built Shelton Hotel. At the time it was one of the tallest skyscrapers in New York. Their suite, high on the 28th floor, had windows facing both north and south. This gave O'Keeffe views of bustling Lexington Avenue, the East River and the vast changing skies above.

PAINTING THE SKYLINE

Thrilled by what she saw, O'Keeffe wanted to capture the vibrant, modern atmosphere of New York. She painted a series of panoramic views of the East River skyline as seen from her apartment, each at a different time of day and in different weather conditions. She also painted portrait-shaped pictures of skyscrapers, including the Shelton, the Ritz Tower and the Radiator Building (right), as well as more mundane buildings. These paintings generally show the buildings close-up, looking upwards from ground level, which helps to emphasise the buildings' great height.

THE PRECISIONISTS

An informal group of American artists, known as the Precisionists, were also inspired by the size and scale of modern American structures. During the height of Precisionism in the 1920s, artists including O'Keeffe, Charles Demuth (1883-1935), Charles R. Sheeler (1883-1965) and Elsie Driggs (1898-1992) depicted new factories, bridges, skyscrapers, locomotives and ships, using flattened forms, dramatic shafts of light and unusual viewpoints to make them seem spectacular. They emphasised geometric lines and shapes, and did not include people in their works.

◄ **Construction work on the Empire State Building in New York in 1930-31. It was for a long time the tallest building in the world.**

TIMELINE ▶

11 December 1924	March 1925	November 1925	December 1925	11 February 1926	June 1927
O'Keeffe and Alfred Stieglitz marry.	O'Keeffe's flower paintings are shown at 'Seven Americans' exhibition at the Anderson Galleries.	O'Keeffe and Stieglitz move to the Shelton Hotel, Lexington Avenue.	Stieglitz opens a new gallery – the Intimate Gallery.	O'Keeffe's first exhibition at the Intimate Gallery.	The Brooklyn Museum, New York, holds the first museum exhibition of O'Keeffe's work.

Radiator Building – Night, New York, 1927

oil on canvas 129.9 x 76.2 cm Fisk University Galleries, Nashville, Tennessee
This painting is one of several depicting a night scene in busy New York City.
Illuminated windows gleam, smoke and steam waft upwards, searchlights scan the
sky, and Stieglitz's name glows in the red neon strip.

'One can't paint New York as it is, but rather as it is felt.'

Georgia O'Keeffe

New York in the 1920s

In O'Keeffe's time, the city of New York was rapidly changing. With the end of World War I in 1918, New York prospered as never before. More and more people came to the city to find work, as new machines replaced many jobs on farms and in rural areas. The city grew into a sprawling, modern industrial metropolis with a fast-growing population. Towering new concrete, steel and glass office blocks defined the skyline of the dense grid of Manhattan streets. These included such landmarks as the Chrysler Building which was completed in 1929.

DEVELOPING CITY

At the same time, new networks of water pipes, sewers and power lines were constructed underground, providing homes and offices with electricity, running water and central heating. By the end of the decade, the number of cars in use in New York City had increased to more than half a million. New roads, bridges and tunnels were built to cope with the flow of traffic.

▲ Police destroying barrels of beer during Prohibition in the 1920s.

PROHIBITION

In 1920 the American government prohibited the making, selling and drinking of alcohol. They hoped to reduce violence and poverty and improve people's health and quality of life. However, Prohibition turned out to have the opposite effect. Throughout the 1920s, people drank more than ever, flocking to new illegal clubs, called 'speakeasies', which were often under the control of criminal organisations and gangsters. By 1925, there were more then 100,000 speakeasies in New York. Despite this, Prohibition was not abolished until 1933.

ENTERTAINMENT

People queued around the block at cinemas to see their favourite stars in the latest Hollywood movies. At the time, movies were 'silent' – the story was conveyed through captions. Sound was introduced in the late 1920s. The biggest stars were Charlie Chaplin, Buster Keaton, Mary Pickford, Douglas Fairbanks and Rudolph Valentino.

Jazz was all the rage and so were dance crazes – the tango, the black bottom and the charleston. Dance marathons, where people danced non-stop for 45 hours or more, became very popular.

By the end of the decade, many people had purchased a newly-available wireless and a gramophone. For the first time people could listen to the latest news and music in the comfort of their homes.

▲ A movie still showing Charlie Chaplin in *The Gold Rush,* 1925.

CHANGING LIFESTYLES

In 1920, American women won the right to vote for the first time. More young women began going out to work, so they had money of their own and increasing independence. Many became 'flappers'; they cut their long hair into short bobs, wore loose knee-length dresses and make-up, which shocked their parents. They also enjoyed drinking and socialising together in groups – activities previously considered unsuitable for women.

THE WALL STREET CRASH

The gaiety and spirit of New York came to an abrupt end in October 1929 when the Wall Street stock market crashed. Thousands of investors lost all their money as the value of shares tumbled. The crash heralded the beginning of the Great Depression (1929-33), when millions of people lost their jobs and lived in great hardship.

◀ Two 'flappers' dancing the charleston on a roof in 1926.

Discovering new inspiration

▲ The art patron Mabel Dodge Luhan, c. 1910.

ARTISTS IN TAOS

Ever since the late 19th century, artists had been going to Taos, a small town mainly inhabited by Indians, on a high, sagebrush-covered plateau. By the 1920s, there was an established artists' colony, with its own Society of Artists, gallery, art materials shop and summer art school.

Mabel Dodge, a rich and forceful art patron, had come to Taos from New York and married Tony Luhan, an Indian from the nearby pueblo (town). She invited artists, writers, journalists, photographers and film makers to stay with her. Her guests included the writers D.H. Lawrence (1885-1930) and Willa Cather (1873-1947), and the photographer Ansel Adams (1902-84).

In the summer of 1929, O'Keeffe wanted to find new inspiration for her painting. Accepting an invitation from the art patron Mabel Dodge Luhan (1879-1962), O'Keeffe set off with a girlfriend to Taos in New Mexico (a southern state of the USA). She was overwhelmed by the vast scale of the unspoiled, dry landscape, the clear light and the extraordinary colours of the bare, rounded mountains. She said, 'It makes me feel like flying.'

O'Keeffe spent her time exploring the area on foot or on horseback, camping in the wilderness or visiting villages and nearby Indian reservations. She learned to drive and bought her own car so she could travel further afield.

▲ The Spanish Mission Church at Ranchos de Taos, built around 1776.

YEARS OF INSPIRATION

O'Keeffe was so taken with New Mexico that she bought a house there and revisited it almost every summer for the following 20 years. During the next few visits, she painted some of the cultural sights of the area, such as the Spanish mission church at Ranchos de Taos and the Taos pueblo (see pages 28-29).

TIMELINE ▶

April-August 1929	December 1929	April 1931	December 1931
O'Keeffe goes to New Mexico for the first time.	Five works by O'Keeffe included in 'Paintings by 19 Living Americans' at the Museum of Modern Art in New York.	Whitney Museum of American Art buys its first work by O'Keeffe.	O'Keeffe's exhibition of 33 New Mexican paintings opens in New York.

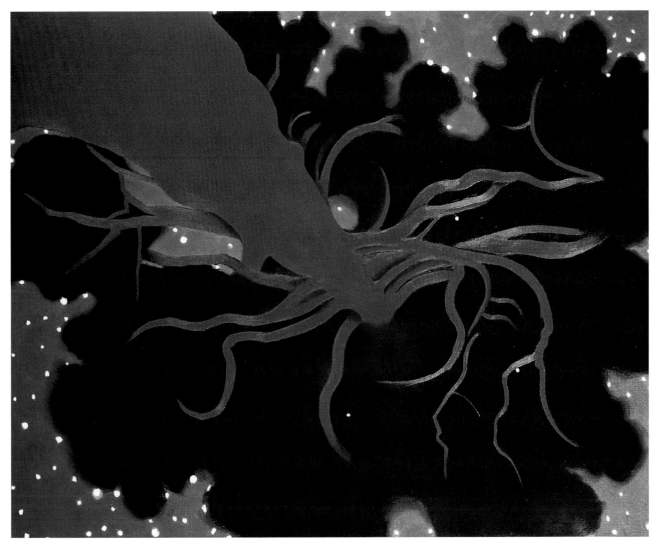

The D.H. Lawrence Pine Tree, 1929

oil on canvas 78.7 x 99.4 cm Wadsworth Atheneum, Hartford, Connecticut

One of the first pictures O'Keeffe painted in New Mexico was based on a pine tree in the courtyard of a house owned by the British author D.H. Lawrence, under which he used to write. The unusual angle of the tree trunk is the foreshortened view that O'Keeffe saw when she lay underneath the tree on a carpenter's bench.

*'… you lie under it on the table – with stars –
it looks as tho' it is standing on its head.'*

Georgia O'Keeffe

New Mexico

▲ The sagebrush-covered land around Taos.

In the 1920s and 1930s, New Mexico was an unspoiled desert wilderness. There were no major roads through the high, dry, sparse land. The old Spanish towns were small and quiet, with narrow dirt roads, lined with low buildings. There were very few cars and people travelled in horse-drawn wagons and used mules for carrying heavy loads.

▶ A Native American folk dance at a pueblo in New Mexico.

PUEBLOS

There were numerous Indian pueblos (towns), each with its own laws, customs and ceremonial days. O'Keeffe visited many of these to watch public ceremonies and dances. She painted several pictures of one particular pueblo – the one at Taos.

TAOS

Taos Indians have lived in New Mexico for almost a thousand years. The centre of their pueblo is a large plaza where celebrations and dances are held. The sacred creek which runs through the plaza is the pueblo's source of drinking water. Tall wooden structures in the plaza are communal racks used for drying corn, meat and berries. The beehive-shaped adobe mounds are communal ovens, known as 'hornos', where people bake bread and pies.

TAOS HOUSES

The individual dwellings (made of adobe – see page 34) are stacked one on top of the other, four storeys high. Each door is the entrance to a different home. People who live in the upper storeys reach their homes via ladders. In the past these were pulled up in times of danger or during enemy raids.

◀ The stacked Taos houses with a beehive oven and drying racks in the foreground.

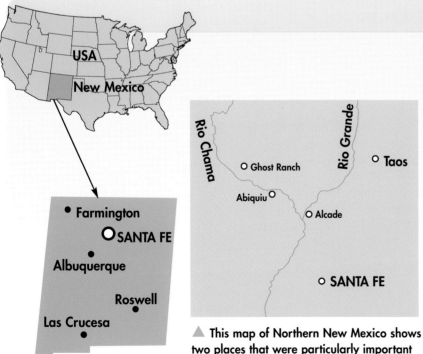

▲ This map of Northern New Mexico shows two places that were particularly important to O'Keeffe – Ghost Ranch and Abiquiu where she bought homes.

NEW MEXICO

New Mexico became the 47th state of the USA in 1912.

New Mexico is renowned for its varied scenic beauty. To the north rise the Rocky Mountain ranges, in the south stretches the Sonoran Desert, to the east lie the Great Plains and in the west are spectacular canyons. The Rio (river) Grande runs straight through the middle. The incredible geographic diversity is accompanied by a vast variety of flora and fauna.

The art traditions of New Mexico are rich and varied as well – a mix of Native American, Hispanic and contemporary. Today, the northern region is a major centre for contemporary art. Santa Fe, in particular, has hundreds of galleries and artists' studios.

Skulls and bones

◀ O'Keeffe holding a pelvic bone, c.1930s, Ansel Adams. Stieglitz was not the only famous photographer to take pictures of O'Keeffe. Adams is famous for his photographs of the American landscape.

THE WHITE PLACE

O'Keeffe was fascinated by the variety of landscapes she discovered in New Mexico. One of the strangest sights she painted was the 'white place', where there are rows of startling columns that look like castle towers (see below). Formed over millions of years from whitish volcanic ash and mud, the columns have been eroded by wind and water, creating strange shapes and folds. O'Keeffe painted several views of the white place, in different lights and from various distances.

After O'Keeffe's first few trips to New Mexico, she shipped back to New York a barrel of sun-bleached bones from the desert. She had collected skulls of horses, cows, elks and rams, as well as thigh bones and ribs. For O'Keeffe, these hard, dry bones were a powerful symbol of the harsh, barren, but beautiful desert, and reminded her of New Mexico at times when she could not be there.

PAINTING BONES

The first pictures O'Keeffe made of bones showed a single, enlarged skull. This was set against a flower, a feather or the colours of the American flag. Later, she combined her three main interests (landscapes, flowers and skulls) into one picture, rather like a collage, to sum up her experience of New Mexico (see right).

O'Keeffe used bones as a motif in her paintings for many years and decorated her homes with them. She painted a series of 'pelvis' pictures, using the empty socket of an animal's pelvic bone as a white frame for a view of the sky, the moon or a landscape.

▲ The striking rock formations of the 'white place'.

TIMELINE ▶

February 1932	August 1932	January 1933	February 1933	Spring 1934	Summer 1934
O'Keeffe exhibits her first bone paintings.	O'Keeffe goes on her first trip outside the USA on a painting trip to Canada.	Exhibits 'Paintings Old and Some New' at An American Place in New York.	O'Keeffe falls ill and cannot work for the rest of the year.	Metropolitan Museum of Art buys its first O'Keeffe picture – *Black Hollyhock, Blue Larkspur*.	O'Keeffe's first summer at Ghost Ranch.

Ram's Head, White Hollyhock – Hills, 1935
oil on canvas 76.2 x 91.4 cm Brooklyn Museum of Art, New York
Here, the huge ram's skull takes pride of place in the centre, hovering in mid-air. The tips of its long, twisting horns reach almost to the top corners of the canvas, stretching across the hills of the Rio Grande Valley where the ram once might have grazed.

'The bones seem to cut sharply to the centre of something that is keenly alive in the desert tho' it is vast and empty and untouchable – and knows no kindness with all its beauty.'

Georgia O'Keeffe

Desert views

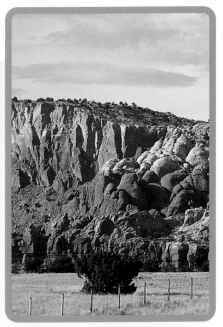

▲ The cliffs around O'Keeffe's ranch dominate the skyline and appear in many of her paintings.

O'Keeffe's home in New Mexico was initially a house on Ghost Ranch, in the Chama River Valley. Behind it was a wall of pink and yellow-coloured cliffs, while in front there was an open plain of sparse shrubland. Groves of cottonwood trees grew nearby and, in the distance, she had a view of the Pedernal mesa (a broad, flat-topped rocky hill).

MOUNTAIN LANDSCAPE

The mountain landscape soon became the most important subject that O'Keeffe wanted to paint. She not only painted the views that she could see from her windows, but also drove long distances to paint in remote areas beyond the reach of dirt roads. Her favourite spot was some bare, remote hills about 240 kilometres from Ghost Ranch, which she nicknamed the 'black place'.

ROCK FORMATIONS

The rock formations at Ghost Ranch are made of different geological layers in a riotous display of colour. The top layer is sandstone, shale and coal, and underneath it lie mudstones. Both were deposited by a swamp a hundred million years ago. Below these is a layer of grey gypsum and below that is a wide layer of pink, windblown sandstone. At the bottom are mounds of siltstone.

▲ O'Keeffe painting in her car, 1937, Ansel Adams. She used the car as a makeshift studio, sitting in the back and swivelling the front seat, so it could support a canvas. The car also sheltered her from the fierce sun, dusty wind and unexpected bursts of rain.

TIMELINE ▶

January 1936	May 1938	February–April 1939	October 1940	January 1943
The first exhibition showing just O'Keeffe's New Mexico paintings.	O'Keeffe receives an honorary doctorate from the College of William and Mary, Williamsburg.	O'Keeffe travels to Hawaii to paint promotional pictures for the Dole Pineapple Company.	O'Keeffe buys a house on eight acres at Ghost Ranch.	First major O'Keeffe retrospective at the Art Institute of Chicago.

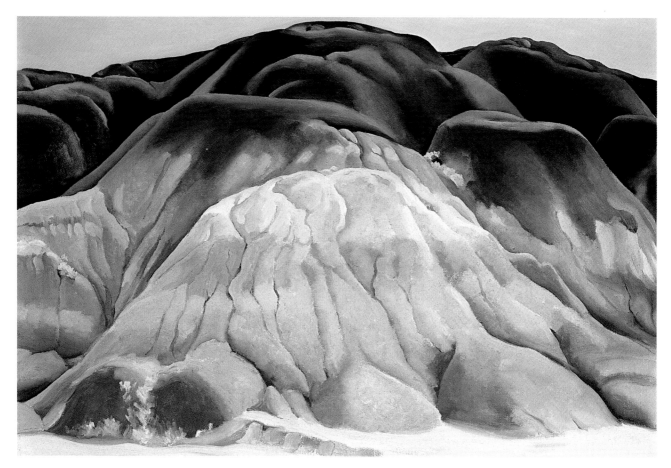

Grey Hills, 1942

oil on canvas 76.2 x 99.1 cm Indianapolis Museum of Art, Indiana

At first O'Keeffe painted these bare, grey hills from some distance away and included some ground and sky, as in this picture. She quite precisely depicts the folds and clefts of the rugged hillside. Later, she focused on one particular cleft in the hills as seen from close up. She painted a series of dramatic views using strong, flat contrasts of light and dark.

'Those hills. They go on and on – it was like looking at two miles of grey elephants.'

Georgia O'Keeffe

An adobe home

▲ You can just see the ends of the log roofs poking through the tops of these stacked adobe buildings.

ADOBE BUILDINGS

Hundreds of years ago, Pueblo Indians made their homes by covering rocks or woven branches with a mixture of mud and straw, known as adobe. The Spanish who later arrived in the area introduced wooden moulds, into which they poured the adobe and left it to dry in the sun. The adobe bricks were fixed together sideways to make thick walls, which were coated outside with mud plaster. Inside, the walls were plastered with a mixture of sand, mud and straw and polished with sheepskin. The roof was made with logs, called vigas, with split cedars laid on top. These were covered with sagebrush and a layer of earth.

In the small village of Abiquiu, a few miles from Ghost Ranch, O'Keeffe found her ideal house, which she purchased in 1945. Made of adobe (see panel), it was set high on a hill with spectacular views of the Chama River Valley and the hills beyond. It had a large, fertile garden with its own water supply so O'Keeffe could grow fruit, vegetables and flowers. She continued to split her life between New York, with Stieglitz in the winter, and New Mexico, alone in the summer.

RENOVATION

When O'Keeffe bought the house there were two buildings, both in ruins. She converted one, previously the pigsty, into her studio, bedroom and bathroom, furnishing them entirely in white. The other, larger building housed the kitchen, living and dining rooms, and more bedrooms.

PERMANENT MOVE

Stieglitz died in 1946 and O'Keeffe was busy for three years settling her husband's estate. In 1949, she moved permanently to New Mexico, spending the winters and spring in Abiquiu and the summer and autumn at Ghost Ranch.

► O'Keeffe's house in Abiquiu. The feature that fascinated O'Keeffe most about the house was the painted wooden door that punctuated a long, plain wall in the inner, open-air courtyard.

TIMELINE ►

31 December 1945	14 May 1946	13 July 1946	1946-1949	Spring 1949	1949	February 1951
O'Keeffe buys her house at Abiquiu.	Museum of Modern Art, New York holds an O'Keeffe retrospective.	Stieglitz dies.	O'Keeffe settles Stieglitz's estate in New York.	O'Keeffe moves to New Mexico for good.	O'Keeffe is elected to the National Institute of Arts and Letters.	O'Keeffe travels to Mexico. Meets artists Frida Kahlo and Diego Rivera.

Patio with Clouds, 1956

oil on canvas 91.4 x 76.2 cm Milwaukee Art Museum, Wisconsin, gift of Mrs Edward R. Wehr

O'Keeffe used the door of her house as a central image in over 20 paintings and drawings, contrasting its dark, rectangular shape with the warm, sandy colour of the adobe wall. In these pictures, the shapes are mainly geometrical. The door and wall are flattened and have very little detail or texture.

'I bought the place because it had that door in the patio. . . I had no peace until I bought the house.'

Georgia O'Keeffe

Travelling the world

THE RIO GRANDE

The Rio Grande, one of the rivers O'Keeffe painted from the air, flows 3,030 kilometres due south from southern Colorado all through New Mexico to the Gulf of Mexico. For centuries, it has been the area's main source of water for farming. Most pueblos are situated along this river or its tributaries. In the past, as mountain snow melted in the spring, the river banks overflowed, depositing rich minerals on the land. This earned the river the nickname 'the Nile of the southwest'. Dams have now been built along the river, so this annual flooding no longer happens.

▲ O'Keeffe visited Machu Picchu, in Peru, in 1956. She said, 'I've never seen nature so absolutely terrifying.'

In 1953, when O'Keeffe was over 60, she made her first journey by plane. For the next 30 years, she travelled all over the world – to Europe, Latin America, the Far East, North Africa, the Caribbean, Southeast Asia and the Middle East.

VIEWS FROM ABOVE

However, O'Keeffe painted scarcely any pictures of the particular places she visited. Instead, she was fascinated by seeing how different the world looked from the great height of an aeroplane – the simplified patterns and shapes, and the contrasting colours of rivers, roads and fields. These inspired her to draw and paint a series she called *Rivers Seen from the Air*.

The infinite expanse of sky and the puffy banks of white clouds seen through the plane windows also excited O'Keeffe. She used these images to create enormous paintings of the vast horizons of the sky. The largest, painted when O'Keeffe was 78 years old, measures 3.8 metres high by 11.3 metres wide. The canvas was too big for her studio, so she painted it in her double garage, working from early morning until dusk all summer long.

▲ The Rio Grande seen from above is quite spectacular.

TIMELINE ▶

Spring 1953	Spring 1956	Spring 1959	October 1960
O'Keeffe goes on her first trip to Europe – visiting Spain and France.	O'Keeffe spends two months in Peru and the Andes.	O'Keeffe goes on a three-month world trip, visiting India, Southeast Asia, Pakistan, the Middle East and Rome.	An O'Keeffe retrospective is held at Worcester Museum of Art, Massachusetts.

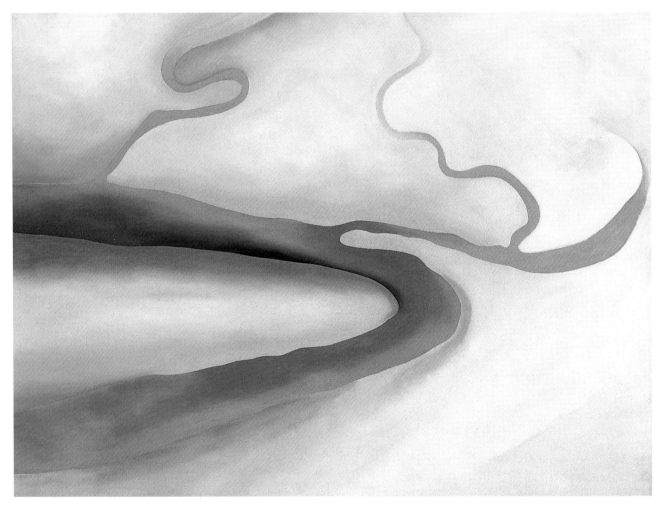

It was Green and Blue, 1960
oil on canvas 76.4 x 101.9 cm Whitney Museum of American Art, New York
O'Keeffe painted more than a dozen huge aerial views of rivers winding through barren lands, from a bird's-eye perspective. She was struck by the beauty of the clear-cut patterns and shapes that she had seen from aeroplanes.

'It is breathtaking as one rises up over the world one has been living in. . . and looks down at it stretching away and away.'

Georgia O'Keeffe

A ripe old age

▲ O'Keeffe with a clay pot at Abiquiu in 1974. She was excited to be creating things again and had a kiln built at Ghost Ranch for firing her pottery.

A LIVING LEGEND

By her old age, O'Keeffe had become a major celebrity. She was the subject of a television documentary, and the book she wrote about her work, called simply *Georgia O'Keeffe* and published in 1976, was a bestseller in America. Reproductions of her paintings started appearing on book covers, greetings cards and as posters. After she died in 1986, her house at Abiquiu was made a National Monument and a museum of her work was opened in Santa Fe in 1997. It is the only museum in the United States devoted to a single woman painter.

During her travels, which continued throughout the 1960s, O'Keeffe collected shells, stones and other natural treasures. She used the black rocks collected on a rafting trip she made down the Colorado River in 1961, at the age of 74, for her painting, *Black Rock with Blue III* (see right).

FAILING EYESIGHT

Tragically, in 1971, O'Keeffe began to lose her eyesight. It worsened so quickly that soon her world was blurred and shadowy. She could no longer see the things she loved most – particularly the landscape – so she stopped painting.

She employed a young assistant, Juan Hamilton (b. 1945), to help her. At first he just did odd jobs, but he soon became a trusted friend. He was a potter-sculptor and taught O'Keeffe how to make hand-rolled pots. Hamilton also encouraged her to start painting again with the help of assistants. Towards the end of O'Keeffe's life, Hamilton helped her prepare a book and plan a major exhibition of her work. At the age of 96, she went with him on her last trip abroad, to Costa Rica.

O'Keeffe died aged 98 in Santa Fe. At her own wish, her ashes were scattered from the top of the Pedernal mesa (see page 32), the place she had claimed as her own and loved for so long.

◀ From her house at Ghost Ranch O'Keeffe could see in the distance the Pedernal mesa, where her ashes were scattered.

TIMELINE ▶

1962	October 1970	Autumn 1971	Autumn 1973	1976	November 1977	6 March 1986
O'Keeffe is elected to the American Academy of Arts and Letters.	An O'Keeffe retrospective is held at the Whitney Museum of American Art.	O'Keeffe's eyesight begins to worsen.	O'Keeffe takes up pottery, encouraged by her assistant, Juan Hamilton.	O'Keeffe publishes a book about her work.	A TV documentary about O'Keeffe is broadcast.	O'Keeffe dies in Santa Fe, at the age of 98.

Black Rock with Blue III, 1970

oil on canvas 50.8 x 43.2 cm The Art Institute of Chicago

Here, a single, glossy stone almost fills the canvas. O'Keeffe has painted it so that you can't tell whether it is an enormous boulder or an enlarged pebble.

'The black rocks... seem to have become a symbol to me – of the wideness and wonder of the sky and the world.'

Georgia O'Keeffe

O'Keeffe's legacy

Georgia O'Keeffe is a major American artist of the 20th century. She painted American subjects, such as New York skyscrapers, Western landscapes and flora. She tried to create a fresh and deliberately American style, which was not influenced by the European art tradition.

'I think... that I am one of the few who gives our country any voice of its own.'

Georgia O'Keeffe

STYLE AND COLOUR

O'Keeffe simplified objects and landscapes, leaving out unnecessary details. She used strong colours, so that things appeared far more intense than they were in real life. She also isolated and magnified single objects, often making them larger than life so that they filled the canvas, appearing almost abstract.

Another of her innovations, influenced by photography, was to telescope space, so that things seem either very near or very far away. Critics view O'Keeffe as a forerunner of the American abstract art movement known as colour-field painting – where canvases are filled with wide expanses of colour.

▲ *Charter,* Ellsworth Kelly, 1959.
O'Keeffe felt that the work of Ellsworth Kelly, a leading colour-field painter, had a great deal in common with her own. She once said, 'Sometimes I've thought one of his things was mine.'

THE IMPORTANCE OF NATURE

O'Keeffe's quest was to establish an original visual language to express her feelings and experiences, as well as her reverence for the power of nature. One of her main themes was the grandeur and vastness of the American landscape, but she was also inspired by single, small natural objects.

'I have picked up seashells and rocks and pieces of wood. . . I have used these things to say what is to me the wideness and wonder of the world I live in.'

Georgia O'Keeffe

MODERN WOMAN

Perhaps an equally important part of O'Keeffe's legacy is the role model she provided for women artists – her way of life as a modern, independent woman as much as the timelessness of her art. In the 1970s, many women artists who felt neglected and frustrated by the art world viewed O'Keeffe as their heroine. They admired her dedication, self-reliance and self-discipline.

Unusually for a woman growing up in the early part of the 20th century, O'Keeffe did not become a mother and housewife, but single-mindedly dedicated her life to painting, producing a huge number of works. Even though she married, as she grew older, O'Keeffe deliberately chose to spend increasing amounts of time living and working on her own in a remote place. At the time, this was considered dangerous and most unusual for a woman.

FOLLOWING O'KEEFFE

Judy Chicago (b. 1939), a leading feminist artist, included O'Keeffe in her sculptural work *The Dinner Party*, a symbolic history of women's achievements in history. She and other women artists saw O'Keeffe as 'the mother of us all'.

> *'Her work provides a foundation upon which we can build a universal language to express our own point of view as women.'*
>
> Judy Chicago (artist)

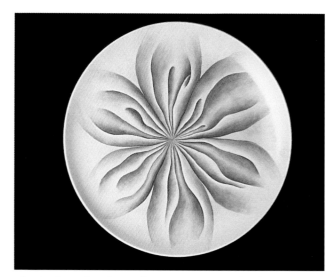

▲ 'Sophia' plate from *The Dinner Party,* Judy Chicago, 1979. *The Dinner Party* is a triangular work of art, 15 metres on each side, with numerous different parts including ceramics, china painting and needlework. O'Keeffe, among hundreds of women, is honoured in the work and the Sofia plate reflects her style.

O'KEEFFE MUSEUM

O'Keeffe is the only woman in the USA to have a museum dedicated solely to her works. The Georgia O'Keeffe Museum in Santa Fe opened in 1997. It has a permanent collection of more than 120 of O'Keeffe's paintings, drawings and sculptures. There is a changing selection of these works on exhibition throughout the year.

Other exhibitions present works by artists or photographers who worked at the same time as O'Keeffe, or show her work alongside the work of other modern American artists.

▲ The Georgia O'Keeffe Museum in Santa Fe, New Mexico.

Sharing a love of nature

Throughout their lives, O'Keeffe and Stieglitz regularly wrote letters – both to each other and to other artists, photographers and writers, as well as to relatives and friends. One of their regular correspondents was Arthur Dove, a key artist in the Stieglitz Circle.

Like O'Keeffe, Dove had a passionate love for nature and, like her, he tried to create a new visual way of recording his feelings about it.

◀ Dove wrote to Stieglitz about O'Keeffe in 1916 when he first saw her charcoal drawings.

> *That girl is doing without effort what all we moderns have been trying to do.*

▼ Stieglitz wrote to Dove on 18 June 1918, describing his reaction to O'Keeffe.

> *She is much more extraordinary than even I had believed. In fact I don't believe there ever has been anything like her. Mind and feeling very clear – spontaneous – and uncannily beautiful – absolutely living every pulse-beat.*

ARTHUR DOVE

Dove (1880-1946) was the first American abstract painter. During his lifetime he was little recognised and he sold very few of his paintings. He had to work as a magazine illustrator to support himself. He never had a major exhibition of his work in a museum or gallery.

Dove played a leading role in the fight to give artists a royalty fee for the reproduction of their work.

▲ A portrait of Arthur Dove by Alfred Stieglitz in 1911.

TIMELINE ▶

1887	1905	1912	1916	1918	1922
15 November 1887 Georgia O'Keeffe is born on a farm in Wisconsin, USA.	**1905** Studies at the Art Institute of Chicago.	**1912** Works as an art teacher in Texas.	**1916** Charcoal drawings exhibited. Begins to work using watercolours. Heads the art department in Canyon. Works are included in a group exhibition at 291.	**1918** Leaves her position at Canyon as a result of catching 'flu. Moves to New York. Spends her first holiday at Lake George. Father dies in an accident.	**1922** Paints at Lake George, including first large landscapes.
1892 Attends Town Hall School.	**1906** Struck down with typhoid.	**1914** Enrols at Teachers' College in New York. Studies under Dow.			**1923** Solo exhibition of 100 of her pictures at the Anderson Galleries.
1898 Begins taking drawing lessons.	**1907** Enrols at the Art Students League in New York.	**1915** Starts teaching art in South Carolina.	**1917** First solo exhibition at 291 – she sells her first charcoal drawing.	**1919** Begins using oils.	
1903 Enrols at Episcopal Institute.	**1908** Works as a commercial artist.			**1921** Exhibition of Stieglitz photographs of O'Keeffe.	**1925** Flower paintings exhibited. Moves to Shelton Hotel.

EXTRACTIONS

Dove was one of the first artists to create purely abstract paintings, although they were inspired by the basic shapes of plants, animals and landscape forms (see page 17). He called these paintings 'extractions', since he thought they were a way of showing the essential energy of nature. O'Keeffe admired Dove's work and bought several of his paintings. She wrote to Stieglitz that Dove was the only American artist who is 'of the earth'.

▼ For several years, Dove lived on a houseboat, so he could capture the changing light and movement of the sea and sky. He wrote to Stieglitz about his experience of a storm.

It is now 3:45am in the midst of a terrific gale and we are anchored in the middle of Manhasset Bay. . . have been trying to memorise this storm all day so that I can paint it. Storm green and storm grey. It has been too dark and nerve-strained to paint.

I wish you could see what I see out the window – the earth pink and yellow cliffs to the north – the full pale moon about to go down in an early morning lavender sky behind a very long beautiful tree – covered mesa to the west – pink and purple hills in front and the scrubby fine dull green cedars and a feeling of much space – it's a very beautiful world – I wish you could see it.

▲ Many of O'Keeffe's letters were equally direct about the colours, shapes and wonder of nature she experienced. While living at Abiquiu in September 1942, she wrote enthusiastically to Dove.

1926	1931	1934	1940	1956	1973
1926 First exhibition at the Intimate Gallery.	**1931** Exhibition of 33 New Mexican paintings opens.	**1934** First summer at Ghost Ranch.	**1940** Buys house at Ghost Ranch.	**1956** Two months in Peru and the Andes.	**1973** Takes up pottery, encouraged by her assistant Juan Hamilton.
1927 The Brooklyn Museum, New York, holds her first museum exhibition.	**1932** Exhibits her first bone paintings. Goes on a painting trip to Canada, her first trip outside the USA.	**1936** The first exhibition showing exclusively New Mexico paintings.	**1945** Buys house at Abiquiu.	**1959** Three-month world trip.	**1976** Publishes a book about her work.
1929 Goes to New Mexico. Five works included in exhibition of 'Paintings by 19 Living Americans'.	**1933** Falls ill and cannot work for a time.	**1938** Receives an honorary doctorate from College of William and Mary.	**1946** Stieglitz dies. **1949** Moves to New Mexico for good. **1953** First trip to Europe.	**1961** Rafting trip down the Colorado River. **1971** Eyesight begins to worsen.	**6 March 1986** Dies, in Santa Fe, at the age of 98.

Glossary

abstract: art that does not imitate the world around us. It is usually impossible to recognise objects, people or places in abstract art.

adolescence: the time between childhood and adulthood.

charcoal: a drawing stick, usually made from burned wood. It can be easily smudged and produces a good range of tone and a soft-edged effect.

composition: an artistic arrangement of parts of a painting or the subjects for a photograph.

feminist: someone who wants equal rights for women.

geometric: having regular lines and shapes.

gramophone: a machine that plays records.

gypsum: a natural hard white substance.

harmonious: where the different elements of something work well together as a whole.

Impressionists: a group of artists based in Paris during the late 19th century who painted 'impressions' of the world with broad brushstrokes of pure, unmixed colour. The group included Auguste Renoir (1841-1919), Claude Monet (1840-1926) and Edgar Degas (1834-1917).

life model: someone who poses for an artist, usually without clothes.

mesa: an isolated flat-topped hill with steep sides.

metropolis: a large city.

oil paint: a type of paint made by mixing pigments (made by crushing plants or minerals) with linseed oil. Oil paint can be applied thick, straight from the tube, or it can be thinned (diluted) using white spirit or turpentine.

panoramic: a picture of a wide, uninterrupted landscape.

patron: a person who gives financial support to someone else.

prairie: a large area of grassland, which usually does not have trees and is found in North America.

Prohibition: the period in America (1920-33) when alcohol was not allowed to be made or sold.

pueblo: a North American Indian town or village.

retrospective: an exhibition showing an artist's development over his or her lifetime.

sagebrush: a shrubby strong-smelling plant.

shale: a soft rock that splits easily, originally formed from mud or clay.

silkscreen print: a colour printing process. A stencil is cut and placed on a fine mesh, attached to a wooden frame. Paint is squeezed through the unmasked areas on to a piece of paper underneath.

still life: a picture of objects, usually carefully arranged by the artist.

suffragette: a woman who seeks the right to vote through organised protests.

typhoid: an infectious fever which causes red spots and sickness.

viewpoint: the place from which a picture is painted.

watercolour: a painting created with colours (called pigments), diluted with water. Lighter tones are achieved not by adding white paint, but by adding water.

Museums and galleries

Nearly all of O'Keeffe's works are exhibited in museums and galleries in the United States. Most of the ones listed here have a wide range of other artists' works on display.

Even if you can't visit any of these galleries yourself, you may be able to visit their websites. Gallery websites often show pictures of the artworks they have on display. Some of the websites even offer virtual tours which allow you to wander around and look at different paintings while sitting comfortably in front of your computer!

Amon Carter Museum
3501 Camp Bowie Boulevard
Fort Worth, Texas 76107-2695
www.cartermuseum.org

The Art Institute of Chicago
111 South Michigan Avenue
Chicago, Illinois 60603-6110
www.artic.edu/aic

Carl Van Vechten Gallery
Fisk University Galleries
18th Avenue North
Nashville, Tennessee 37208
www.fisk.edu

The Cleveland Museum of Art
11150 East Boulevard
Cleveland, Ohio 44106
www.clevelandart.org

Georgia O'Keeffe Museum
217 Johnson Street
Santa Fe, New Mexico 87501
www.okeeffemuseum.org

The Metropolitan Museum of Art
1000 Fifth Avenue at 82nd Street
New York, NY 10028-0198
www.metmuseum.org

Milwaukee Art Museum
700 N. Art Museum Drive
Milwaukee, WI 53202
www.mam.org

Museum of Fine Arts, Boston
Avenue of the Arts, 465 Huntington Avenue
Boston, Massachusetts 02115-5523
www.mfa.org

The National Gallery of Art
6th Street and Constitution Avenue, NW,
Washington, DC 20565
www.nga.gov

Philadelphia Museum of Art
Benjamin Franklin Parkway and 26th Street
Philadelphia, PA 19130
www.philamuseum.org

San Francisco Museum of Modern Art
151 Third Street
San Francisco, CA 94103-3159
www.sfmoma.org

Whitney Museum of American Art
945 Madison Avenue at 75th Street
New York, NY 10021
www.whitney.org

Index